# Writers – How To Publish Free

## E-Book and Self-Publishing Formatting

## Linda Felberbaum-Meckler

# Copyright

©    Writers- How To Publish Free 2015 Updated <u>2020, 2021</u>

All Rights Reserved to Linda Felberbaum – Meckler


No part of this book shall be reproduced or transmitted in any form or by any means Electronic, mechanical, magnetic, photographic including photocopying, recording, or by any information storage retrieval system.

Contents

Copyright ............................................. 2
Disclaimer ........................................... 9
The Writers Decision ....................... 12
Introduction ........................................ 1
Why I Wrote This Book ...................... 1
E-Books .............................................. 4
Insert Pictures/Art .............................. 6
Self-Published Books ........................ 7
Audio Books ........................................ 8
Microsoft Word ................................... 9
From Writer to Publisher ................. 11
What Do I Do With My Manuscript? . 13
Part 1 ................................................ 14
E-Books ............................................ 14
Book Title ......................................... 17
Book Subtitle .................................... 19
Book Cover ...................................... 20

Instructions ........................................ 21

Formatting Your Manuscript. ............ 21

Page Layout ..................................... 22

No - No Formatting .......................... 24

Positive Formatting ......................... 25

What's Under Category? ................. 26

Creating The Table Of Contents Automatically .................................... 32

Reference Information ..................... 34

Create One Document ..................... 35

Search Button .................................. 40

The First Step ................................... 41

Creating A Template ........................ 42

Book Editing and Writing ................. 49

Editing: ............................................. 52

Stripping Formatting ........................ 54

Note Pad Software ........................... 55

Paragraphing .................................... 56

Part 2 .................................................. 60
Inserting Pictures/Art ........................ 60
Picture Tools ..................................... 65
Moving A Picture .............................. 70
Picture Locked In Place ................... 71
Picture Tools/Sizing ......................... 72
Creating Book Covers ...................... 73
Saving Your Book ............................ 76
Saving as PDF ................................. 77
www.amazon.com ............................ 78
E-Book Websites ............................. 80
Part 3 .................................................. 81
Self-Publishing ................................. 81
Self-Publishing Story ....................... 83
What Size Book ................................ 87
ISBN Numbers ................................. 90
Creating A Template ........................ 92
Page Layout ..................................... 101

Header/Footer ................................106
Book Finished ...............................109
Interior File .....................................111
Create A Cover ..............................113
Free Marketing ...............................115
Social Networks ............................119
Public Speaking ............................122
You are an expert on:.....................123
Copyright........................................126
Other Documents: .........................128
Part 4..............................................129
Audio Books ...................................129
www.acx.com .................................129
Keystrokes Short Cuts ...................132
Linda Meckler's Books ...................135
**More Fiction:**...............................137
**Relationships:** ............................140
**How To Books:** ..........................141

Phone Numbers ............................. 145
Websites Listed ............................. 145
Table of Contents Update Reminder
..................................................... 147

Motto

**Think with your brains**

**Not your emotions**

Linda Felberbaum-Meckler

**Disclaimer**

I would like to make a statement that I cannot prove the table of contents will work on every Electronic appliance or on every website you upload your Electronic book.

I cannot guarantee the sale of your books on the websites I have given you. The marketing of your book is up to you. When uploading and E-book or paperback book it costs zero money and whatever you make is a definite income.

Microsoft Word is explained for teaching purposes only.

Your ISBN number is important in how you make the correct selection to keep complete control over your book publishing. Read carefully.

Linda Felberbaum-Meckler

Biography

**Linda Felberbaum-Meckler** Is an Author, Public Speaker, Editor, Book Publisher, Ghost Writer and Book Consultant

Linda is an author of approximately thirty Fiction and Non-fiction books. She teaches classes in E-book and Self-Publishing Formatting. After teaching several classes she decided to write this book. Linda's students keep teaching her. She never stops learning.

## The Writers Decision

An author said to me once and this has stuck with me to this day.

*"Only you can make the decision to publish your own work. If you don't have confidence in yourself, nobody else will."*

*It is scary for someone else to read your work at first. You will get over it. Don't let that stop you from becoming an Author and Book Publisher.*

**Writers How To Publish Free**

# Introduction

# Why I Wrote This Book

When I started to write I was just like you, excited and dreaming about the time I would be a great author and make mountains of money.

My problem was I didn't have a starting place. I had never met an author in my life. I didn't have any networking connections made and I was at a complete loss as to what my first step should be.

My book, Writers - How To Publish Free, gives all writers a chance to publish their own writing. Their choice is electronically by an E-

### Linda Meckler

Book or by Self-Publishing which is also electronic for FREE.

I want everybody who has written a book to be able to publish their book for free and have complete control over their book publishing.

When you start thinking about an E-book or a Self-Published Book, you should have already written your book.

Your book should be edited and organized.

**The formatting of an E-book is different from a Self-Published book.**

## **Writers How To Publish Free**

### 4 Parts

1. E-Books
2. Inserting Pictures/Art
3. Self-Published Books
4. Audio Books

## Linda Meckler

## E-Books

The **E-book** is compact without any extra line spacing. Think cell phones or other small electronic devices. The font is usually 12 inches

## Writers How To Publish Free

and most often in Times News Roman. Now you can use most fonts.

What makes E-Books so unique is they are "***in the Now and the Future.***" Paper is not involved. E-Books are a fast and efficient way to retrieve information on any subject and read books forever. The world is at your fingertips.

The trees will not be cut down for an electronic book. Paperback books will be a way of the past in the future.

## Linda Meckler

**Wendy Meckler with Ginger**

## Insert Pictures/Art

This part of my book will include the information you will need to insert, move, and size pictures/art.

## Writers How To Publish Free

## Self-Published Books

The Printed Book or it is called, Print On Demand (POD) is formatted for creativity. The spacing in the book can be drawn out.

The formatting in this book will vary to demonstrate to you how you can create your own interior design.

A printed book is still needed for many purposes. Many people have not converted to the E-Book and like to hold a book in their hands.

It is also a marketing tool when giving talks or for education, etc.

Be ready to follow the instructions in this book to format and upload your **Self-Published Book.**

**Linda Meckler**

# Audio Books

I will give you information on Audio Books. This is another way to publish Free. www.acx.com this is part of www.amazon.com.

Audio Creation Exchange.

## **Writers How To Publish Free**

## **Microsoft Word**

I will be using Microsoft Word 13 to instruct you on how to format your E-books and your Self-Published books.

There are many versions of Microsoft Word. The arrangements of different headings may vary but if you keep searching you will find what you are looking for.

In this book I list all the categories and most of the headings under each category. This should help you when trying to find a specific heading.

### Linda Meckler

**Writers**
**When you format your books by yourself, you have complete control over your book publishing. You can change your book and cover over and over again for FREE.**

Think about this. Complete freedom for the writer and publisher. You own all the rights to your books.

## Writers How To Publish Free

### From Writer to Publisher

Being an author is a special feeling in which your self-esteem will soar and you will find yourself smiling from the inside out.

Being a Self-Published Author, you must have a marketing plan. Some books fit into the category of being easier to market than others.

When your book is Self-Published it will not automatically be placed in a bookstore for sale. The reason for this is shelf space. The '***established publisher'*** pays for shelf space in the bookstores for their authors.

### Linda Meckler

There are other places to sell your books **on www.amazon.com, and <u>www.barnesandnoble.com</u>**. There are other websites but these are the largest. When you finish this book, you will have learned **Microsoft Word.**

There is another website which is large and sells books. It is www.smashwords.com. The formatting for this website is different and more complex. The instructions for book formatting are not in this book.

www.smashwords.com does not have phone support.

## Writers How To Publish Free

## What Do I Do With My Manuscript?

*Does it sit in my computer until it crashes?*

*Create an E-book?*
*Create a Self- published book?*

*Why not both?*

*Then add an Audio Book.*

## Linda Meckler

### Part 1

# E-Books

**Write an E-book as often as you change your socks.**

lol   (Laugh Out Loud)

**E- Books** can be downloaded to various kinds of electric devices. Most of them are small.

In creating your Electronic book, I will be using Microsoft Word 2013.

This is set up on a ribbon. When you look across the top of the screen it will look like this.

## **Writers How To Publish Free**

There are now newer versions of Microsoft Word. It is constantly changing. The basic parts to the Software Program will be there but it might be under a different heading. They have probably made some structural changes to the up-dated versions.

**The Ribbon**

**File**
**Home**
**Insert**
**Design**
**Page Layout**
**References**
**Mailings**

## Linda Meckler

**Review**

**View**

**Help**

## Writers How To Publish Free

## Book Title

    When you write your e-book, the title is important.

## Linda Meckler

It must have what the book is about. What is the focal part of your story?

**What is wrong with this book title or subtitle?**

The title is confusing.

There is no subtitle.

Three books in one is confusing. I didn't self-publish this book myself; I went to a publisher who charged me big bucks. Now I know how to do it myself and it costs ZERO.

**Be very specific.**

Make the title short and to the point. **Example**: Ghost Kids. This is why when selecting the title be sure

## Writers How To Publish Free

you have thought of every word combination.

    Don't worry. If you make a mistake in the title selection it can be changed.

### Book Subtitle

## Linda Meckler

What is the book about? Be specific.

**Subtitle: Hate Bullying**

The title is broad. It needs to be more specific about what aspect of basketball is addressed.

The **subtitle** gives the book more specific information.

### Book Cover

The book cover is also important. Create a book cover in an eye-catching color and design.

Many people think the book cover is more important than the title. Sometimes it is if your book is lined up with others. In this case it may or may not be important.

## Writers How To Publish Free

### Instructions
### Formatting Your Manuscript.

I will put the **heading** on the top of each instruction.

*If your book is uploaded onto the website and it does not look correct go back to your original document make your changes and upload it again. It's Free and unlimited.*

## **Linda Meckler**

## **Page Layout**

Page Layout

Margins

Custom Margins (bottom of Page)

**Paper**

5" Wide

8" Length

Click on Okay

**Margins**

1 inch from top

0.76 inches inside (Right)

0.76 inches (Left)

1 inch bottom

0.14 inches Gutter Right

## **Writers How To Publish Free**

6 " wide

9" long

1 inch top

0.75 inches inside (Right)

0.75 (left)

1 inch bottom

0.15 Gutter - Right

You will see the entire document will change size.

This will be the size of your book. When you read a book, this is usually the dimensions of the book you are reading.

Have you ever read a book where the words run off the page? Or if they are

## Linda Meckler

in the crease of the book and hard to read? This is what this is for. To get the best reading space possible on the page. If it needs an adjustment. Adjust.

**No - No Formatting**
**Never use the Tab Bar.**

**Leave 1 -2 line spaces between paragraphs.**

**Insert**

Do not use Bullets

There are bullets in this book because it will be a printed book.

## **Writers How To Publish Free**

The bullets will be removed when converted to an E-Book. You are the author you make this decision.

**Positive Formatting**

**Insert**

Use Page Breaks when you are changing chapters.

You can use numbering.

Make sure all of your sentences are completed by wrapping them. It means the computer will do it itself.

### Linda Meckler

If you stop it in the middle, your sentence in your book will stop in the middle.

**Example**: If you stop
in the middle,
your sentence in your book
will stop in the middle.

Do you see the difference?

### What's Under Category?

Not every item is listed under each category. In some Microsoft Word Programs it could be different.

## Writers How To Publish Free

**File**

Save
Save As
Open
Close
Recent
New
Print
Save and Send
Options
Exit

**Home**

Different Fonts Styles
 (Using Arial)
Font Size 14
The font color chart

### **<u>Linda Meckler</u>**

Bold   Italic   Underline

Bolts

Numbering

Styling –Modifies Headings and other parts of the document.

Paragraph Icon  - A map of keystrokes. It has two legs with a line across the top.

Paragraph opens to make selections:

Indenting

Line Spacing

Don't add space between paragraphs of the same style

## Writers How To Publish Free

Editing - Find, Replace, Select

## Insert

Cover Page

Blank Page

Page Break

Insert Table

Insert Picture

Clip Art

Shapes

Smart Art

Chart

Screenshot

Hyperlink

Bookmark

Cross-reference

Header

**Linda Meckler**

Footer

Page Numbers

Text Box

Quick Parts

Word Art

**Design**

Themes

**Page Layout**

Margins

Orientation

Size

Columns

Breaks

Line Numbers

Hyphenation

## Writers How To Publish Free

Water Color

Page Color

Page Borders

**References**

Table of Contents

Insert Footnote

Insert Index

**View**

Print Layout to screen

Full Screen Reading

Web Layout, Outline, Draft

Ruler, Gridlines

Navigation Pane

## Linda Meckler

## Creating The Table Of Contents Automatically

**Home**

Click on the page you want the Table of Contents on. (TOC)

**Change Styles.**

Choose the Heading you want to use.

Example: Heading 1, Title

Highlight the titles or chapter names.

Click on the heading you want to use.

**References**

Click on Table of Contents

## Writers How To Publish Free

Your Table of Contents will set-up on the page you selected.

**View**

**Navigation**

When you complete the Table of Contents now you can click on View and click on navigation.

On the left side of your screen your table of contents will open up and you can follow it throughout your document.

## Linda Meckler

### Reference Information

Put contact information for your readers to contact you on every social media book, etc. as possible. Your contact information should include, a website address, e-mail or any blogs you have. This is important.

## Writers How To Publish Free

Example:
**www. facebook.com lindafelberbaummeckler**

Other options are authorlindameckler I decided I had two names my maiden name and my married name. I decided to use my maiden name as much as I can now for marketing. Hey people I'm a Felberbaum.

### Create One Document

You cannot format and create a manuscript if you have files saved in various files throughout your computer. All your documents must be in one file. Read below how to accomplish this:

### Linda Meckler

These three important symbols are located in the top right-hand corner of your screen.

A **dash -** To move the page to the bottom or minimize.

**Square** To reduce the size of the page - in the middle.

**X Symbol** - Closes the document.
**Click on the dash –**
**Home**

Open the document you want to use. Now save it and click on the dash – at the right top of the screen.

## **Writers How To Publish Free**

This will minimize your document and place it on the bottom of your screen.

Next open another document you want to add to your present document.

Click **Control A** to highlight the entire document.

Right Click Copy

This will make a copy of your entire document.

Minimize it and then click on the first document you minimized.

It will once again open up.

**Linda Meckler**

Right click for paste.

You are now on your way to creating one document.

Save

Continue with this method until all the documents are copy and pasted into your first document.

Now you can copy, paste and edit.

Your book is now on its way to becoming published.

**Home**

## Writers How To Publish Free

**Paragraph Button on Home**

Click on the paragraph button. It looks like the symbol for paragraphing when typewriters were once used or two vertical lines with a horizontal line across the top.

With this button turned on you will see some interesting things.

It will give you a map of every keystroke you have made in your entire document.

This is important to format your document correctly.

## **Linda Meckler**

It will show paragraphing, every space in a word, spacing after periods, etc. When you edit your book, you can check for errors.

**Search Button**
**Home**

It's called a search button but it looks like a question mark. You can always ask Microsoft Word how to find anything at any time. It will open up websites for you to explain what you want to know.

It is located at the top of the screen under the X.

# __Writers How To Publish Free__

## The First Step

Change

The

Margins

## Linda Meckler

## Creating A Template

When you create a template to use for your E-Book it will be easy to copy and paste all of your headings and chapters into this template.

**Page Layout**

Margins

**Custom Margins**

**Paper**

5 Inches Wide    8 Inches Length

Your margins should be set-up correctly.

## **Writers How To Publish Free**

**Page One**

**Home**

The Title of the book
The Subtitle of the book.
Authors Name

**Insert**

Page break

**Page 2**

**Home**

Copyright Page

## **Linda Meckler**

You can write what you want as long as you have:

All rights Reserved.

The title of the book

Author's name

The year it was copyrighted or written.

© The copyright symbol.

**Insert**

Page Break


**Page Three**

# Writers How To Publish Free

## References

Table of Contents

## Insert

Page break


## Page Four

## Home

Acknowledgment

## Insert

Page Break


## Page Five

## Linda Meckler

### Home

A blurb: Why I wrote This Book

Introduction

From The Author or Combine both (Heading)

Introduction

### Insert

Page Break

### Page Six

### Home

### Author Biography.

This can be at the end of book the book or beginning. It can include the Authors Picture. Your education

## Writers How To Publish Free

and expertise on the book you have written.

**Insert**

Page Break

**Page Seven**

**Home**

## Linda Meckler

# Writers How To Publish Free

## Book Editing and Writing

**Fiction Books**

When I started writing years ago, I didn't have any idea on how to edit a fiction story. I had to start from the beginning.

I learned by hearing criticism from friends and family about a mistake in grammar or whatever.

When I started teaching my class on E-Book Formatting, I was surprised to learn my students didn't have any idea on how to edit a book or what was required to edit a book.

## Linda Meckler

They also didn't know how complicated writing a fiction book was.

I wrote the book, Editing Fiction, Mistakes because of me.

Thousands of writers out in the world can take advantage of this unusual book on editing and fiction writing.

## Writers How To Publish Free

**Non – Fiction Books**

Non-fiction is written completely different. You don't have to worry about characterization, quotation marks or any other fancy punctuation.

You do have to have your facts and documentation correct.

**Editing your book is extremely important.**

**Things to be considered when you edit your book:**

### Linda Meckler

## Editing:

1. Organization.
2. No repeating if possible.
3. Are your characters believable? You will need a detailed description and a purpose throughout the book for each character.
4. Is the story line easy to understand?
5. Grammatically Correct?
6. Punctuation Correct?
7. Verb Tenses Correct?
8. **Read your book out loud to yourself or to somebody else. In this way you can hear if any words were left**

**out or if the story flows easily.**

9. If your book is Science Fiction keep it in the Science Fiction Mode.
10. If your book is in another era. The book needs to reflect this era. Cell Phones, computers, airplanes or cars were not around in the 1800's.
11. Etc.

## Linda Meckler

### Stripping Formatting

If you are having trouble uploading to the websites because of Electronic Squelching (electronic interference) problems try this method. The software used should be in your computer. It is called **Note Pad**. Search for it.

If not click on **Change Styles** at the top it will give you an option to **clear all the formatting.**

Your book will not upload correctly to the websites, or will not come out as the finished product you were looking for if there is Electronic Squelching attached.

The software which is used by Amazon and Barnes and Noble is

## Writers How To Publish Free

highly technical and will not accommodate Electronic Squelching.

### Note Pad Software

Copy and paste your document into Note Pad. It removes all the formatting and the electronic squelching.

You will see it will be a plain document not like the one you just pasted into it.

It removes all the spaces between lines.

The pages numbers will be gone.
The pictures will be gone.

## Linda Meckler

Copy and paste into a new Microsoft Word page.

You will have to start book formatting from scratch.

### Paragraphing
**Home**

On the ribbon in the middle you will see the word paragraph.

There is a **small arrow** next to it on the right.

Click on the arrow. A text box will open up.

## Writers How To Publish Free

Make your selection of the 3 choices on how you want to start your paragraphs.

This box is very important. If set up correctly, you can format your book in one easy step.

**None –**
There will not be an indention at the beginning of the paragraph.

**First Line –**
　　　There will be an indention at the beginning of the paragraph.

**Hanging –**

## Linda Meckler

The first words in the paragraph will hang over.
Play with these three selections to see how they work in your paragraphing.

When you make that selection, your document will change.

**Remove** the extra space between paragraphs go to the same arrow. Click on it.

You will see a box that says

Don't add space between paragraphs of the same style. Click on that.
**Line Spacing** is in this box.

## Writers How To Publish Free

Click on the spacing you desire.

**Single**

1.5

Double

At Least

Exactly

Multiple

**Control A** - When you highlight your entire document and go to the paragraph box, you can format your entire document at this time.
For an E-Book spacing is precious. Don't have any extra lines or spaces anywhere. Keep everything snug and together. This is why you use your **page break** to change a chapter or etc. Think small electronics.

## Linda Meckler

# Part 2

## Inserting Pictures/Art

**Insert**

Click on Pictures or Clip Art

Height 2.78 inches  Width 3.25 inches

**Height 2.44"  Width 3"**

**Insert**

## Writers How To Publish Free

When you want to insert pictures to your document follow these steps:

**All pictures or art work must be a JPEG.**

## Linda Meckler

**2.81" High – wide 3"**

**Insert**

**Click on pictures or clip art.**

You will be given the option to click on the picture you want to use.

## **Writers How To Publish Free**

Save as: On the desktop for easy access.

The cursor must be on the spot you want your picture to be inserted. Depending upon the size of your book

**2.51 height, width 3.34**

your picture needs to be sized correctly for the page size.

**Home**

## Linda Meckler

Keep each picture on its own line. You can also format the pictures differently by clicking on the pictures and click on wrap text. There are several ways to place your picture in the document.

Placing a picture on a line may make it change pages.

### Picture Tools

On the right side of the screen will be a place where you can change the size of the picture. **You want the picture locked in.**

## Writers How To Publish Free

Do not drag to make larger or smaller. It must be locked in or it can float when up-loaded onto the websites.

If you are inserting a colored or black and white picture the resolution must be **300 for a printed book or the picture will not be able to be as sharp and bright as you will want.**

In order to get the image to 300 resolution Click on picture tools to the right.
If you have photo shop elements you can follow these instructions:

Your resolution needs to be 300 pixels for the printed image to be at its best.

## Linda Meckler

This is for black and white and colored photos/art.

Photoshop Elements 9 and 13

**Edit**

In Photoshop Elements go to image.

Size the picture to 3.25 if this is the size you want or something similar.

When placed in the book or any document click on the picture.

Click on picture tools at the top of the computer.

## __Writers How To Publish Free__

At the right you can adjust the picture size. Do not drag.

Where it says resolution - Type in 300.
**Save as** and place your photo on the desk top for easy access.
You might have to practice a few times to get this correct.

When you are clicked on a picture in Microsoft Word.
Picture Tools will open up.
Click on **compress pictures**.

All these different steps should give you the 300 resolution.

Other Software

### Linda Meckler

If you have access to software which will change the resolution size, make sure the resolution is at 300. Make the photo 100%. There are many different software programs and they work differently.

**For an E-Book photo the resolution only needs to be 72.**

## Writers How To Publish Free

## Moving A Picture

Click on the picture.

This will open a bounty box

The box around the picture

Right click.

Click on format picture

Click on layout

Click on **tight.**

Now you can move the picture.

Moving the picture in a document stumps many people now you have the answer.

## Linda Meckler

### Picture Locked In Place

Repeat the same instructions above for moving a picture.

Instead of clicking on tight click on **top and bottom**. In this way your picture will stay where you have placed it on the line.

There are many positions you can place the pictures in.

The information on pictures I have given you, some of it is not readily available.

## Writers How To Publish Free

## Picture Tools/Sizing

- For sizing open up picture tools.
- It's part of Microsoft Word.
- On the right side you can change the height and width of the picture.
- Lock the size in.
- Do **not** drag the picture to make smaller or larger.

- **Photo Shop Elements 9 or 13**
- Go to the Image menu bar.
- Click on Image Size

## Linda Meckler

### Creating Book Covers

- If you have a book cover - use it.
- Scan it into your computer.
- The size varies 1000 x 1600 or could be larger.
- Have a professional make you one.
- Download software from the Internet or buy it and make your own.
- **Microsoft Word.**
- You cannot save your cover as a JPEG.
- Print it.
- Scan it into the computer. It will now be a JPEG.
- **Google Images.**

## Writers How To Publish Free

- You can use these free or they have ones that have a charge.
- Be careful with copyright infringement.
- Use your own pictures or art work.
- Microsoft Publisher.
- Quick Publications
- Save as a JPEG.
- Photo Shop
- Cover Creator

  k**dp.amazon.com (Amazon Will own your cover)**

- The sizing of the cover can vary from website to website.

## **_Linda Meckler_**

- If the cover is not large enough when you upload to the websites the correct size will be flashed.
- Resolution 300 pixels in colored/Black and white in a printed book.
- **Microsoft Pictures**
- It is also part of Microsoft Word and can be used to size pictures.

## Writers How To Publish Free

### Saving Your Book File

**Save as**: It will save your book in documents. It will ask for file name.

Give it a name. **Example**: Art Book Save as a Microsoft Word Document.

Save as: It will save your book on the desktop if selected.

**Note:** Sometimes when you open your saved book on the desktop it doesn't always save the last corrections.

## Linda Meckler

### Saving as PDF

At the bottom of the screen when you Save As: Under **File name** is a tab which asks you to save many ways.

When converting to PDF choose PDF. Make sure you keep a copy which has not converted to PDF if you want to make changes.

Now you are ready to upload your book onto the Amazon Kindle website.

For an E- book <u>do not</u> convert to a PDF file

## Writers How To Publish Free

**www.amazon.com**

You will need to have a log in for

**www.amazon.com**

For E books the website is:

kdp.amazon.com

Follow the prompts.

**Page 1**

You do not need an ISBN number.

One will be assigned to you.

Need a book cover.

Upload cover first

Upload book next.

There will be numerous questions for you to fill out on both pages.

## Linda Meckler

You will be asked for banking information the first time you upload a book.

**Have this information ready:**

Checking or Savings Account Number

Bank Tracking Number

Social Security Number

Credit Card or ATM Card Number

In this way the money from the sales of your books goes directly into your bank account.

**Writers How To Publish Free**

**E-Book Websites**

**Amazon**

You need to have a log on to **www.amazon.com.** 1-866-216-1072

The E-Book website is: **kdp.amazon.com**.

When you are using the **kdp.amazon.com** webpage.

You can track your book sales.

**<u>Linda Meckler</u>**

## Part 3
## Self-Publishing

Change A Self-Published book as often as you change your clothes

lol (Laugh Out Loud)

(POD) Print on Demand

## Writers How To Publish Free

When you have completed the formatting and cover of your printed book, don't worry if you want to make changes the charge is zero.

Go back to your original document in your computer. Make your changes and then up-load again.

You are in complete control of your books!!! Hold your book in your *hands and say, "I created this book!"*

## Linda Meckler

### Self-Publishing Story

I did what most of you would have done. I did a computer search for websites for self-publishing companies.

One caught my eye and I decided to contact that company. I even made a trip to the publishing company in another state and met the editor. The company was small with few people.

I paid $700.00 and I thought my book was going to be published. I dreamed of holding my book in my hands.

What happened was the company was sold and my book was never published. I had to fight with the

## Writers How To Publish Free

publishing company to get my money back.

Two years later I decided I wanted to publish my book. This time I approached the subject with my head not my emotions.

I started going to marketing, meetings and conferences. I learned what the word networking meant.

**I asked questions:**

☐ **Questions:**

1. Who published your books?
2. What is the name of your Publisher?
3. How much did it cost?
4. Did it include a cover?
5. Did it include an ISBN number?

## Linda Meckler

6. How long did it take to receive the blue copy of my book back? (Editing Copy)
7. Did you like the Publisher?
8. Would you recommend the publisher to me?
9. Can I be my own Book
10. Did the publisher do any marketing for your book

## **Writers How To Publish Free**

**Create Space has been deleted from Amazon. Now the website for both E books and Published books is**

**www.kdp.amazon.com**

This is your book project. You will have complete control over your book, cover and re-writes. Zero charge if you format your book and create your own book cover yourself.

Now is the time to learn how to format your own Self-Published book, become a Published Author and your own Book Publisher.

**Your book starts with the title.**

## Linda Meckler

**Books are printed in the United States and in other countries.**

### What Size Book

What size book will I need? These book sizes are all in inches. The size of your book is determined by the number of pages and by what kind of book it is.

Example: A book of art or photography may require one of the larger book sizes. These are not all the book sizes.

*5 x 8
*6 x 9
8 x 10

## **Writers How To Publish Free**

8.5 x 11

Before you make any decisions on the Layout of your book read the following:

How many pages will be in your book when sized by the correct dimensions?
Black or White. This means pictures or art work.

Colored - This means pictures or art work. A colored book is more expensive but affordable on www.kdp.amazon.com
Use their template. It can be downloaded from their website. Their

## **Linda Meckler**

template is limited and at times frustrating.

This book Writers-How to Publish Free is set up in this way:

5 inches wide

8 inches long

The most popular size of a book is the size I made my book and also:

6 inches wide

9 inches long

The font which I used in this book is Arial and the font size is mostly 14.

Most books are written in Times News Roman in 12 inch font. Can you see the difference?

## **Writers How To Publish Free**

This is in Arial 12. Can you see the difference?

There are literally a hundred plus fonts to choose from. Be careful some font is not free.

When creating the interior of your printed book put your creativity to work in formatting a book which is easy to read, understand and is attractive.

### **ISBN Numbers**

International Standard Book Number (ISBN) They are 13 digits long.

This number is free.

### Linda Meckler

If you use the free ISBN number your ISBN number stays with www.kdp.com.

There are other options.
If you already have an ISBN Number use it.

**www.bowker.com** is a website where you can purchase from one ISBN Number to blocks. See the website. The ISBN number will be yours. 1-800-.662-070.

This would be a good way to go and your book will have more marketing opportunities.

## Writers How To Publish Free

**Read that section carefully before choosing.** You want to keep complete control over the publishing of your book.

### Creating A Template

There are specific instructions on how to create your own template in this book.

Page Numbering.
Section Breaks.
Inserting Pictures colored - 300 pixels.
Black and White 300 pixels
Create a cover from your photo or art work.
There is much more to consider when creating a Self-Published printed book.

**Linda Meckler**

**The first thing:**

**Change**

**The**

**Margins**

## Writers How To Publish Free

**Page Layout**

**Custom Margins**
**Paper**

5 inches wide

8 inches long

**Margins**

1 inch from the top

0.76 inches inside (Right)

0.76 inches (Left)

1 inch bottom

0.14 inches (Gutter - Right)

These margin sizes can vary from the different size of books and how you want it formatted. Also click on **mirrored.**

**Linda Meckler**

**Page Layout**

**Custom Margins**

**Margins**

6 inches wide

9 inches long

1 inch Top

0.75 inches inside Right)

0.75 inches (Left)

1 inch bottom

0.15 (Gutter - Right)

This changes the size of your book. Whatever size you choose this is

## **Writers How To Publish Free**

where you make the margin changes. This may vary.

### Page One

### Home

The Title of book
The Subtitle of book
Authors Name

### Insert

Page break

### Page 2

### Home

### Linda Meckler

Copyright Page

You can write what you want as long as you have. All rights Reserved.

© The copyright symbol.

The title of book and the author's name.

The year it is written or published.

**Insert**

Page Break

**Page Three**

**References**

## **Writers How To Publish Free**

Table of Contents

**Insert**

Page break

**Page Four**

**Home**

Acknowledgment

**Insert**

Page Break

**Page Five**

**Home**

A blurb: Why I wrote This Book

Or From The Author or Combine both (Heading)

## Linda Meckler

Introduction

Page Break

**Page Six**

**Home**

**Author Biography**

It can be at the end of the book or the beginning.

It can include an Author picture.

Always include your education and your expertise on the subject you have written about.

You can write this is third person.

# Writers How To Publish Free

**Insert**

Page Break

**Page Seven**

**Home**

Other Books By Author

List the book titles by themselves.

With the book titles include a blurb about the book.

A picture of the book cover can be included.

**Note:** These pages can be in different order or different headings. They can be in the front or back of book.

**Linda Meckler**

**Page Layout**

**Breaks**

On the page before the first chapter or where you want to start page numbering or a header or footer

**Insert**

**Section Break**

**Next**

**Insert**

**Page Numbers**

**Note:** It might take a few tries to get the numbering correct. (**see section breaks**)

## **Writers How To Publish Free**

There are different things to consider.

The pages are odd and even.

The pages are mirrored.

Page numbers:

On Microsoft 13

Go to the page you want to start numbering 1,2, etc.

On the page before go to the end of the last sentence and

Open up Layout

Breaks

Next Page

### **Linda Meckler**

Go to Insert

Page Number

Choose which format

A box will open

Show Document Text

Odd and Even

Both should be checked

Link to Previous for page 1

And do the same for page 2

The numbering should continue

If not do it again. This can get complicated and when I used Microsoft 10 it was more complicated.

## Writers How To Publish Free

**Insert**

Blank Page (If Needed)

In this part the section breaks and the headers and footers can become complicated.

Do not give up. Keep trying you will understand this process.

Note: In creating a template there are more ways to format your book. These methods would be more complex and are not included in this book.

When formatting your first book you can keep the formatting simple.

## Linda Meckler

When you click on the header or footer a screen will open up. It will ask 3 questions.

1. Different first page.
2. Different odd and even page.
3. Show document text.

This is where you make your choice of how you want to format your headers and footers.

**The headers and footers can be easy or complicated**

## Writers How To Publish Free

When formatting your Self-Published book. You can use many forms of software besides Microsoft Word. InDesign is very popular. There are many free software systems discussed in the community room. When you start reading and asking questions include in your question what kind of software you are using in detail.

### Header/Footer
### Insert

This works almost the same way as book numbering. The only difference is when you go to insert click on the header or footer.

## Linda Meckler

It will ask link to previous and the answer is no.

This will take a few tries to understand.

It means the start and stop of different sections which include:

Headers / Footers and Page Numbering

**Note:** When using headers or footers check out all of the choices first. There are numerous choices and they all do different things. **Example**: Odd and even pages.

## **<u>Writers How To Publish Free</u>**

You can shut the header and footer box by clicking on the **Design button** at the top middle of the page.

When numbering pages and using the headers and footers in Microsoft Word this is where you will find the most problems.

When I first started formatting my books, I was using Microsoft Word 10. Now I am using Microsoft Word 13 and found it easier to place book numbers where I want them to start and finish. In learning new things don't get lustrated. Keep trying and eventually it will work.

## Linda Meckler

There are videos on You Tube which instruct you on how to number pages and headers and footers.

**Book Finished**

**File**

Click on print. (without printing)
It will print for you onto the screen.
You can see it page by page as it is formatted in your book.

This will work anytime you want to see how your book will look when completed.

**Option**: At the bottom of the computer screen is a plus and minus. If you click

## **Writers How To Publish Free**

on the minus your document will become smaller and you can see several pages at one time. This is another way to check the interior of the book.

Save Your Book. **Example**: Art Book
Save As: Microsoft Word Document
Save As: Desktop
**Note: Blank Page**
Sometimes when you are book formatting a blank page can be inserted without you realizing it. If this happens **check the section breaks. When anything unusual happens go back and check the sections breaks.**

## Linda Meckler

This is accomplished by turning on the paragraph button.

Save as PDF file

Keep a Microsoft Copy for changes.

**File**

Save as PDF Document This is optional.

## Interior File

The interior file is your manuscript. It will go through an Electronic scan which will tell you what is correct and what needs to be changed.

## **Writers How To Publish Free**

www.kdp.amazon.com

Go to dashboard.

Click on your book title.

It will give you all the directions you need to upload your book file.

It will also give you step by step instructions on how to register yourself for direct banking.

**Linda Meckler**

## Create A Cover

When you are ready to create your book cover you will go back to the book title and look for **create cover**.

It has different templates you can use. You can use your own artwork or picture in a Self-Published book.

A **back cov**er is required. Write a short blurb about what your book is about.

When you are finished your book will be locked onto

**Electronic Proofer**

The Interior File and Cover File must be uploaded at the same time and locked in.

## **Writers How To Publish Free**

You price your own book.

You can track your book sales.

Create space will ask you if you want an E-book.

The formatting for an E-book is **incorrect** but they will put it up as an E-book for you anyway.

The kdp.amazon.com website will not be completely filled out.

You will be able to see for yourself when you browse through your book on the website.

## Linda Meckler

You will have to go onto it to complete the two forms.

**Format your own E-book and upload it onto the websites.**

You are now a Published Author and Book Publisher soon to have your printed book in your hands.

**Congratulations!**

**Free Marketing**

Ad Words, Search Words, Category

**www.adwords.google.com**

One of the ways your reader will find your book is by searching by ad words or search words and by a category.

## Writers How To Publish Free

When you end your book, you can add all the other books you have published.

You can write a short blurb about each of the books.

You can add pictures of other book covers.

You can add the title and the first chapter of your next book to be published.

**Word of Mouth**

Carry a copy of your book. Show it to your family and friends.

## Linda Meckler

Always have a business card or flyer with you to hand out and leave in appropriate places.

Make a t-shirt with your name and website on it.

Where a cap or hat with the title of your book on it and include a website on where to purchase your book.

Put a t-shirt on your dog and walk around. You are bound to get attention about your dog and your book.

**Book Signings**

Find places to sell your book. Be creative.

## Writers How To Publish Free

**Blogging**

Write Articles On The Internet.

**Example**: www.wordpress.com

**Your own books:**

When you publish your book either an e-book or a paper book you can advertise yourself and your book. Free Advertising. You can do this is the beginning of the book or in the back. You can just list the title of your books or you can put in a picture of the cover or you can do anything you want. It is your book.

### Linda Meckler

In this book my books are listed in the back of the book with a description of what they are about. In other books of mine I have listed them in the beginning of the book without a description. What would you do?

## Social Networks

www.facebook.com

www.twitter.com

www.pinterest.com

www.linkedin.com

www.youtube.com

www.bookbub.com

www.blogger.com

etc.

## Writers How To Publish Free

**Post Interesting;**

Stories/Articles

Videos

 Photos

Artwork

Start a Website

Blog

Have friends and family write about your book on social media.

**Community Events/Planning**
**Journalism**
**Photography – Never** be without a **camera**. Interesting pictures can become a part of your book. They can be uploaded onto your social media websites.

## Linda Meckler

**Videos** – Create your own videos and be aware of what is going on around you.

**Book Trailers –** Learn how to create book trailers for your books. There is software available. **Option**: Have a professional create one for you. Upload onto www.youtube.com, your website, and social medial.

**www.youtube** is waiting for your video.

**Website:**

Create your own website or have a professional create one for you. **Note:**

## **Writers How To Publish Free**

It is important for you to be in charge of your own website to be able to make changes.

Your biography can go in the front or the back of your book. Your readers want to know about you. Add a picture.

Thank your readers for reading your book. List an e-mall address or website where they can contact you.

### **Public Speaking**

You can now give talks to different organizations, clubs and libraries.

## Linda Meckler

**You are an expert on:**

How to write a book.

How to format a book.

How to publish a book.

The subject of your book.

# <u>Writers How To Publish Free</u>

## Toastmasters History

## 1-949-858-8255

A **toastmaster** is a great way to learn how to become a polished public speaker. It will boost your self-confidence. It will help you with your leadership skills and book sales. www.toastmasters.org

March 24, 1905, Toastmasters was created, by Ralph C. Smedley. He was working for the YMCA (Young Men's Christian Association.in Bloomington, Illinois.

Ralph C. Smedley was a director of education. He saw a need for men

## Linda Meckler

in the community to learn how to speak in public, conduct business meetings, plan programs and work on committees.

In 1970 Toastmasters International admitted their first woman, Helen Blanchard who was registered under the name of Homer Blanchard. In 1973 Toastmasters began officially admitting women. In 1985 Helen Blanchard became the first woman International President. To this day Toastmasters is still going strong.www.toastmastersorg/history

## Writers How To Publish Free

### Copyright

1-877-476-0778

1-202-707-3000

Technical Support

1-202-707-3002

Copyrighting is a way to protect your book. **www.copyright.gov**. Create a log in and fill out the form.

If you get confused you can call the copyright office. Be prepared for this to take from 2 – 4 hours if you have to make numerous calls.

The Library of Congress is on the East Coast. Be aware of the time difference.

### Linda Meckler

It is better to copyright your book online. It is less expensive and you receive your certificate faster. Once you pay for your book on line it is copyrighted.

With an E-book you can upload the book or mail a paper copy or CD to the address listed below:

If you have a Self-Published book you need to send two paper copies to:

The Library of Congress

101 Independence Avenue Southeast, Washington, DC 20540.

The books need to be mailed within **thirty days.**

## Writers How To Publish Free

There are tutorials for you to watch. Some of them are from other websites and they charge big bucks to copyright your book. Be careful.

## Other Documents:

Depending upon the state in which you live in, you might need a:

Sellers Permit

Sales and Tax Document

## Linda Meckler

## Part 4

### Audio Books

Audio Creation Exchange

**What kind of voice do you have?**

**www.acx.com**

1-888-396-6347

The Audio book is for people:

Who can't read.

Who are blind.

Do not like to read.

Drive and listen to a book.

Do not have time to read.

## Writers How To Publish Free

## Audio Book

The Audio book is now booming.

**www.acx.com** is another part of

**www.amazon.com**

Audio Creation Exchange

The narrator will be marketing your book also.

If you want to consider narrating your own book these are the things to consider.

- ✓ A sound proof room.
- ✓ A computer
- ✓ Software and be able to edit the software.
- ✓ The correct microphone.
- ✓ Vocal Variety when speaking.
- ✓ Reading at the correct speed.

## **Linda Meckler**

- ✓ Renting a recording studio if needed.

Go onto this website and read as much as you can.

When your Audio Book is finished it will be available on every Electronic device.

## Writers How To Publish Free

### Keystrokes Short Cuts

Control - End - End of Document

Control - Home – Beginning of Document

Control S - Save

Control C - Copy

Control V - Paste

Control A - Highlights the entire document.

Control Home- Will take you to the beginning of your document.

Control End – Will take you to the end of your document.

Control P- Print

## Linda Meckler

**Snipping Tool**

Go to start button and type in Snipping Tool and you can snip out anything anywhere. Fabulous

## Writers How To Publish Free

## Blogs/Articles

Books are purchased where starred.

www.amazon.com             *

www.barnesandnoble.com *

www.smashwords.com      *

www.infinitypublishing.com *

www.ezinearticles.com

www.wordpress.com

www.authorsden.com

www.twitter.com

www.facebook.com

www.linkedin.com

## Linda Meckler

# Linda Meckler's Books

**Fiction**

A Christy and Brad Adventure Series (4) books in the series.

*Book 1 – **Ghost Kids Trilogy**

2 real kids and 2 Ghost Kids have adventures in an old house in La Jolla, CA. Pirates and Pirates Treasure end the exciting story.

*Book 2 – **Bear Thriller**

AKA These titles The Bear Chase, Chopper Down, and the Chase Is On.

## Writers How To Publish Free

Christy and Brad find adventure in the burning woods.

*Book 3 – **Shoot Out At Niagara Falls**

AKA Adventure at Niagara Falls

A day trip to Niagara Falls turns into (3) exciting adventures.

Book 4 – The Girls Vanished AKA Oak Horse Ranch Mystery

Two girls are kidnapped and the mystery is what, why, where and when.

## Linda Meckler

## More Fiction:

### A Basketball Adventure

Are you being bullied at school?

AKA Pixie A Basketball Adventure

### It's a Dog's Life

Narrated by (4) dogs who were left outside by their owners to roam the streets in the evening. Safety rules for dog owners.

### A Shoe Mystery Series/Adult

### *The Bloody Knife

### *The Bloody Mafia

## Writers How To Publish Free

**\*The Bloody Violins**

**Science Fiction:**

**Space Station Mars**

Life on the space station with romance.

**Non-Fiction**:

**\*Fight Your Medical Insurance Nightmares!! Let me show you how**

It explains Medicare Parts A B C D. Sample appeal letters for the consumer to use to get their insurance to pay. It explains how medical insurance works.

Appeals and Collections Letters for Medical Providers

## Linda Meckler

Sample letters for medical providers to use in order for the insurance companies to pay their claims. Or sample collection letters for their patients to pay their bills.

### Photos of San Diego

Pictures I took on an instamatic camera to use for inspiration for drawing or painting.

Editing Fiction Mistakes

The most common errors when writing fiction.

### An Autobiography Series Outline

An Auto-Biography Outline

## **Writers How To Publish Free**

Follow the outline and finish with your biography.

Outline for Parents of Special Needs Children

Outline for Children With Special Needs

**Relationships:**

**People Make Relationships**

AKA

Hot Relationships

Do you want romance in your life?

## Linda Meckler

Do you not want to be taken for granted?

## Make Over Your Self-Confidence

Low self-esteem and take root in childhood. Weed your roots.

## How To Books:

## Family Food Wars

Make your time together special. Meal times do not need to be declared a war.

## Writers How To Publish Free

### *Writers - How To Publish Free

Why pay to publish your book. Learn how to do it yourself. All the websites and phone numbers needed are in this book.

### Make Your Laptop A Desktop

AKA Computer Stations That Work

Why have neck and shoulder pain?

### TTY Communication Book

## Linda Meckler

Many different ways to communicate when you are deaf or mute.

**Sleep Apnea, CPAP Mask, Sleep Study**

The symptoms of Sleep Apnea, Using your CPAP Machine and go through a Sleep Study

## Books Can Be Purchased

**Digital Books**

www.amazon.com

www.barnesandnoble.com

www.smashwords.com

**Free Articles**

## <u>Writers How To Publish Free</u>

www.ezinearticles.com

www.wordpress.com

www.authorsden.com

www.blogspot.com

lindamecklerauthor-artist

Books which are paperback have a star in front of their title.

If you would like to contact me my blog lindamecklerauthor-artist.

Thank you for reading my book. Please check out my other books and articles on other websites. If you like my book Writers-How to Publish Free, please put a blurb on
**www.amazon.com.**

### Linda Meckler

Please let me know if my book worked for you. If you have any suggestions to make it better, etc. I want to hear from you.

Author, Public Speaker, Editor, Ghost Writer, Book Publisher, Book Consultant

**Phone Numbers**
**Websites Listed**

The important websites and phone numbers are listed below:

**www.amazon.com**

1-866-216-1072

**www.kdp.amazon.com**

**Writers How To Publish Free**

E-Books Kindle

Paperback books

No phone number available.

**www.barnesandnoble.com**

1-800-843-2665

E-Books   Nook

Self-Publishing (Print on Demand)

**www.copyright.gov**

1-877-476-0778   1-202-707-3000

Technical Support 1-202-707-3002


**www.acx.com**

1-888-283-5051

### Linda Meckler

Audio Books

**www.bowker.com**

1-800-662-0701

ISBN Numbers

## Table of Contents Update Reminder

**Important:**

1. Use the **REVIEW** Button to check the spelling and grammar of your document. It will not find everything but it a good start.

2. For Navigating throughout your document use the **VIEW** Button. It will

## Writers How To Publish Free

help you get to where you want to be in your document.

3. **REFERENCE** Button Do not forget to update the Table of Contents.

**Note**: Phone numbers and websites change.

Thank you for reading my book. Let me know about your book publishing stories.

Keep me updated on all your writing.

You can contact me on my blog lindameckleurauthor-artist.

**Linda Meckler**

Easy Reference

**Page Layout**

**Custom Margins**

**Paper**

**5x8 Book**

1 inch from the top

0.76 inches inside (Right)

0.76 inches (Left)

1 inch bottom

0.14 inches Gutter – Right

## Writers How To Publish Free

**Page Layout**

**Custom Margins**

**Paper**

**6x9**

1 inch top

0.75 inches inside (Right)

0.75 inches inside (Left

1 inch bottom

0.15 Gutter – Right


For other size books check on www.kdp.amazon.com

**Linda Meckler**

www.ingramcontent.com/pod-product-compliance
Lightning Source LLC
Chambersburg PA
CBHW071759200526
45167CB00017B/503